R. Nakata K. Frazier

Let's Speak English

Pupil's Book 1

Oxford University Press

Oxford University Press
Walton Street, Oxford OX2 6DP

Oxford   New York   Toronto   Madrid
Delhi   Bombay   Calcutta   Madras   Karachi
Kuala Lumpur   Singapore   Hong Kong   Tokyo
Nairobi   Dar es Salaam   Cape Town
Melbourne   Auckland

and associated companies in
Berlin   Ibadan

OXFORD and OXFORD ENGLISH are trade marks of
Oxford University Press

ISBN   0 19 436061 X

© Oxford University Press

First published 1993
Third impression 1994

Cover illustration by Jane Gedye.

Illustrations by David Cain, Kim Wilson Eversz, Maj-Britt
Hagsted, Steve Henry, Sharon Hudak, Anne Kennedy,
Dora Leder, Paul Meisel, Patrick Merrell, Nancy Myette,
Oxford Illustrators, Bob Rose, and Maggie Swanson

Printed in Hong Kong.

Table of Contents

Let's Talk

Hello, I am Andy.

Hi! My name is Kate.

What's your name?

My name is John.

What is your name?
My name is John.

What is = What's

Let's Sing

Andy

Jenny

Lisa

Scott

Kate

John

♪ **The Hello Song**

Hello, hello, hello!
What's your name?
Hello, hello, hello!

My name is John.
My name is John.

Hello, John!
Hello, John!
Hello!

7

Let's Learn

What is this?
It is a ruler.

What is = What's
It is = It's

8

Practise.

a book

a desk

a chair

a ruler

a pencil

a bag

a pen

an eraser

Let's Learn Some More

Is this a bag?
Yes, it is.
No, it is not.

is not = isn't

10

Play a game.

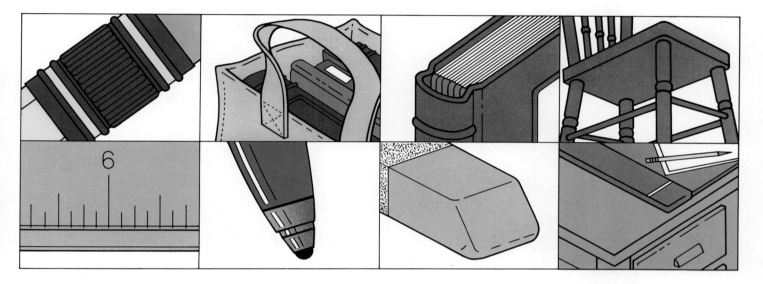

 Let's Learn the Alphabet

♪ **The Alphabet Song**

A B C D E F G H
I J K L M N O P
Q R S T U V W X Y Z

11

 # Let's Move

Stand up.

Sit down.

Open your book.

Close your book.

Point to the teacher.

Touch the desk.

Please be quiet.

Listen carefully.

Let's Listen

1.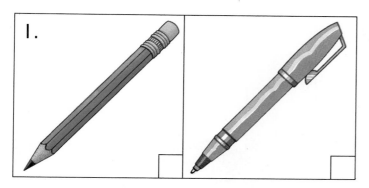

2.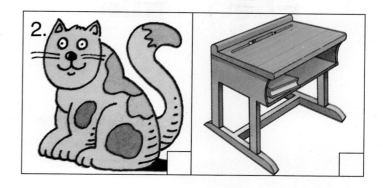

3.

4.

5.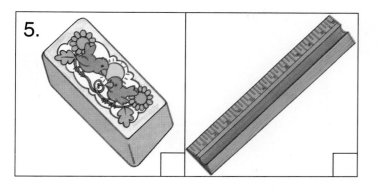

6.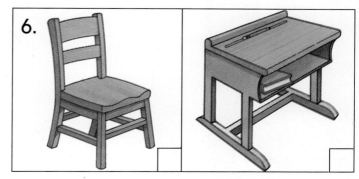

7.

8.

Unit Two

Let's Talk

How are you?
    I am fine, thank you.

I am = I'm

Let's Sing

♪ **Hi, How Are You?**

Hi, how are you?
    I'm fine.
Hi, how are you?
    I'm fine.
Hi, how are you?
    I'm fine. How are you?
I'm fine, I'm fine, I'm fine.

15

Let's Learn

What colour is this? It is red.		It is = It's

16

Practise.

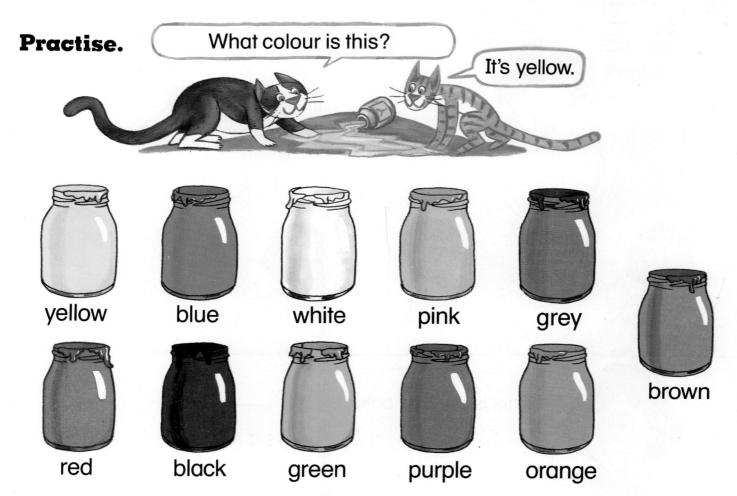

yellow   blue   white   pink   grey

red   black   green   purple   orange

brown

♪ **The Black Cat Song**

17

Let's Learn Some More

This is a blue book.
This is a red and yellow book.

18

Say these.

 Let's Learn the Alphabet

a b c d e f g h i j k l m n o p q r s t u v w x y z

Let's Move

Put your hand up.

Put your hand down.

Take out your book.

Put your book away.

Pick up your pencil.

Put your pencil down.

Write your name.

Look at the board.

apple Aa

20

Let's Listen

1.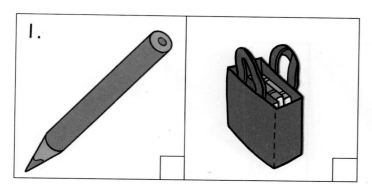

2.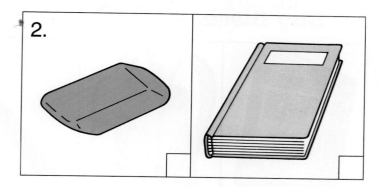

3.

4.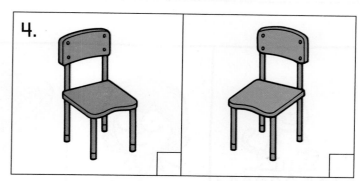

5.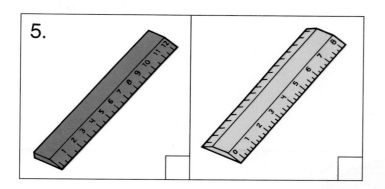

6.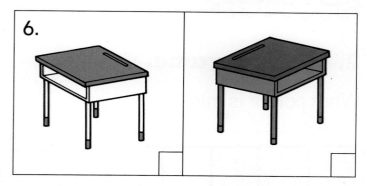

7.

8.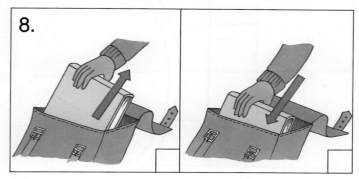

Let's Review

1. Say these.

2. Play a game.

What colour is this?

    It is _____ .

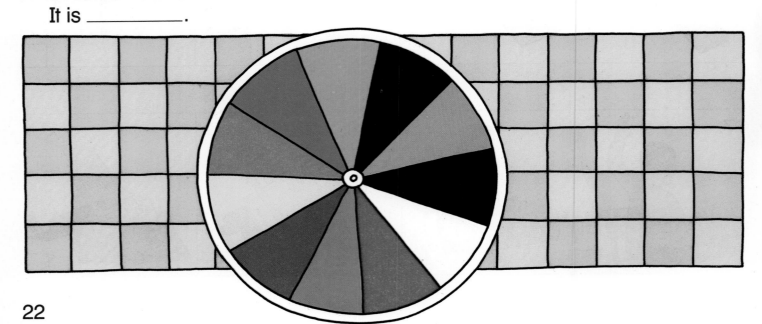

3. Say and act.

4. Ask your partner.

What is this?
Is this a _____ ?

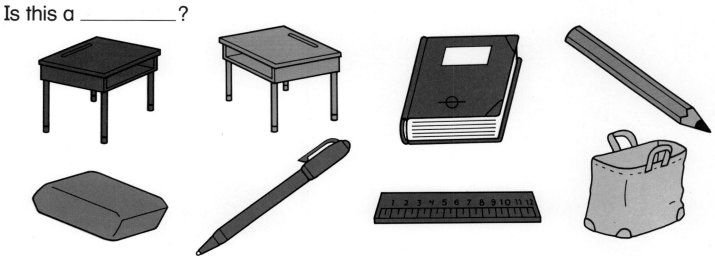

5. Listen carefully.

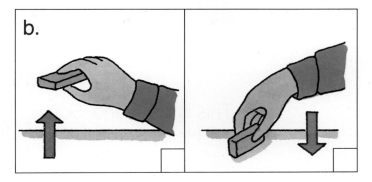

Let's Talk

This is my friend, Sarah.
Hello, Sarah.

Let's Sing

♪ **This Is My Friend**

This is my friend, Sarah.
    Hello, Sarah.
This is my friend, Sarah.
    Hello, Sarah.

This is my friend, John.
    Hi, John!
This is my friend, John.
    Hi, John!

This is my friend, Sarah.
This is my friend, John.
Let's play!

25

Let's Learn

What are these?
They are cassettes.

They are = They're

26

Practise.

a crayon

crayons

a pencil case

pencil cases

a cassette

cassettes

a table

tables

a marker

markers

a notebook

notebooks

Say these.

This is a _____. These are _____.

27

Let's Learn Some More

♪ The Purple Trainer Song

1 one

2 two

3 three

4 four

5 five

6 six

7 seven

8 eight

9 nine

10 ten

How many trainers?

One trainer.	Four trainers.	Seven trainers.

Practise.

A	B	C
a	b	c

Let's Learn the Alphabet

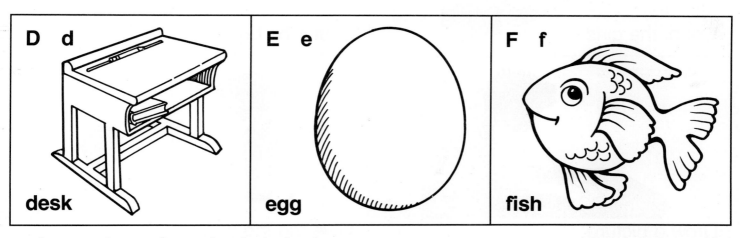

D d · desk

E e · egg

F f · fish

a b c **d** **e** **f** g h i j k l m n o p q r s t u v w x y z

Let's Move

Make a circle.

Make two lines.

Go to the door.

Come here.

Count the girls.

Count the boys.

Draw a picture.

Give me the crayon.

Let's Listen

1.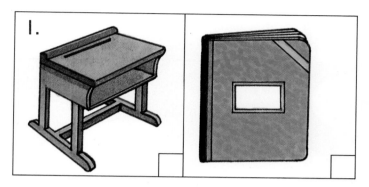

2.

3.

4.

5.

6.

7.

8.

Let's Talk

It is nice to meet you.
It is nice to meet you, too.

It is = It's

Let's Sing

♪ The Family Song

This is my mother.
　Nice to meet you.
Nice to meet you, too.

This is my father.
　Nice to meet you.
Nice to meet you, too.

This is my sister.
　Nice to meet you.
Nice to meet you, too.

This is my brother.
　Nice to meet you.
Nice to meet you, too.

Let's Learn

Who is she?
    She is my grandmother.

Who is he?
    He is my grandfather.

Who is = Who's
She is = She's
He is = He's

Ask your partner.

sister

grandmother

mother

baby sister

brother

father

grandfather

friend

Who's he?

He's my father.

Say these.

_____ is my sister.

_____ is my friend.

Let's Learn Some More

He's tall. She's short.

He is tall.
She is short.

He is = He's
She is = She's

Practise.

He's young.

She's old.

young   old | tall   short | pretty   ugly | thin   fat

36

Guess.

She is old.
She is pretty.
Who is she?

He is short.
He is ugly.
Who is he?

She is my _____.

He is my _____.

He is tall.
He is thin.
Who is he?

She is young.
She is fat.
Who is she?

He is my _____.

She is my _____.

Let's Learn the Alphabet

G g

girl

H h

house

I i

ink

J j

jeans

a b c d e f **g h i j** k l m n o p q r s t u v w x y z

Let's Move

go to sleep   wake up   do your homework   eat your dinner

make a mess   tidy up   watch TV   play the piano

Do not watch TV.

Do not = Don't

Don't watch TV.

Don't make a mess.

Let's Listen

1.

2.

3.

4.

5.

6.

7.

8.

Let's Review

1. Say these.

2. Ask your partner.

Who is he?
Who is she?

3. Say and act.

Hello, Sarah.

It's nice to meet you.

4. Answer the question.

How many _____?

5. Listen carefully.

a.

b.

Unit Five

Let's Talk

How old are you? I am seven years old.	I am = I'm

Let's Sing

♪ **The Happy Birthday Song**

It's my birthday today.
   It's your birthday today.
It's my birthday today.
   Happy birthday, Jenny!

One, two, three, four, five, six,
   Seven years old!

Now I'm seven years old.
   Now you're seven years old.
Now I'm seven years old.
   Happy birthday, Jenny!

43

Let's Learn

| What is it? | It is = It's |
| It is a doll. | |

Practise.

a yo-yo   a kite   a car   a ball   a doll

a puzzle   a robot   a skipping rope   a racket   a bicycle

Guess.
What is it?

Let's Learn Some More

It is little.
It is a little yo-yo.

It is = It's

Say these.

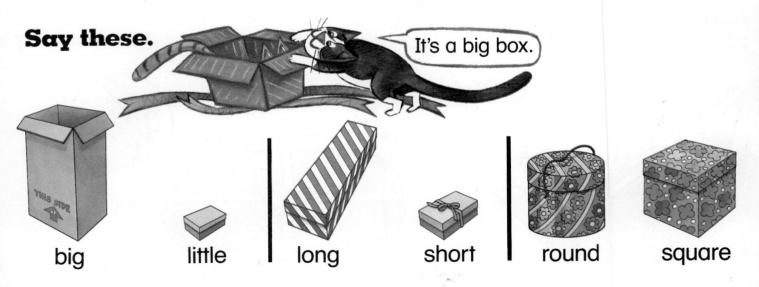

| big | little | long | short | round | square |

Practise.

Is it a pencil?

Yes, it is. It's a long pencil.

 Let's Learn the Alphabet

K k	L l	M m	N n
kite	lion	mother	notebook

a b c d e f g h i j **k l m n** o p q r s t u v w x y z

Let's Move

play with a yo-yo

kick a ball

catch a ball

hit a ball

do a puzzle

skip

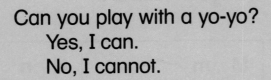

Can you play with a yo-yo?
Yes, I can.
No, I cannot.

cannot = can't

Can you play with a yo-yo?

Yes, I can.

No, I can't.

Let's Listen

1.

2.

3.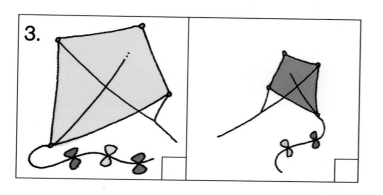

4.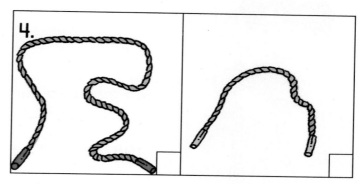

5.

6.

7.

8.

Unit Six

Let's Talk

Is the sun shining?
Yes, it is.
No, it isn't.

The sun is shining.
The sun's shining.

♪ Let's Go Out and Play!

The sun is shining,
the sun is shining.
What a sunny day!
The sun is shining,
the sun is shining.
Let's go out and play!

The wind is blowing.
What a windy day!

Oh look! It's raining.
What a rainy day!

Oh look! It's snowing.
What a snowy day!

Let's Learn

How many clouds are there?
There are six clouds.
There is one cloud.

There is = There's

52

Practise.

Count them.

There is _____. There are _____.

53

Let's Learn Some More

in	on	under	by

Where's the kite?

It's in the tree.

Where are the books?

They're under the table.

Where is the kite?
  It is in the tree.
Where are the books?
  They are under the table.

Where is = Where's
It is = It's
They are = They're

Practise.

Let's Learn the Alphabet

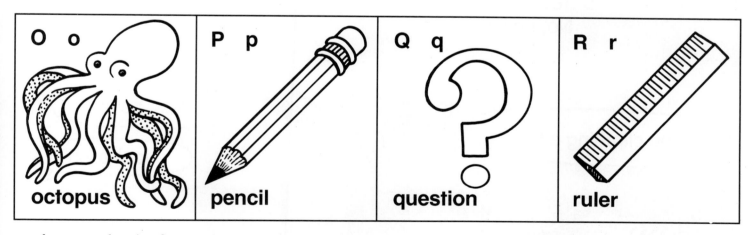

O o	P p	Q q	R r
octopus	pencil	question	ruler

a b c d e f g h i j k l m n **o** **p** **q** **r** s t u v w x y z

55

Let's Move

He's climbing a tree.

They're playing tennis.

He's reading a book.

She's playing tag.

She's riding a bicycle.

He's flying a kite.

Is he climbing a tree?
Yes, he is.
No, he isn't.

is not = isn't

Is he climbing a tree?

Yes, he is.

No, he isn't.

Let's Listen

1.

2.

3.

4.

5.

6.

7.

8.

Let's Review

1. Say these.

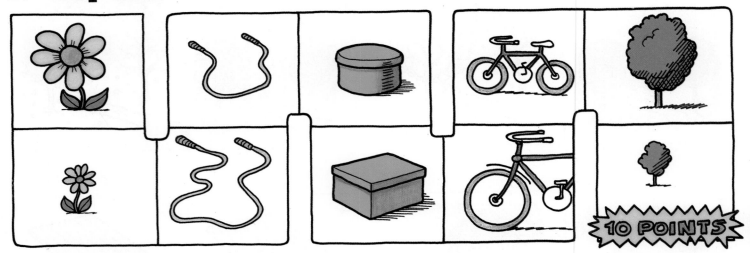

10 POINTS

2. Answer the question.

How many _____ are there?

3. Say and act.

How old are you?

?

No, it's raining.

58

4. Ask your partner.

Can you _____?

Yes						
No						

5. Listen carefully.

Where is it?

Let's Talk

Here you are.
Thank you.
You are welcome.

You are = You're

Let's Sing

♪ **Peaches, Apples, and Plums**

Peaches, apples, and plums.
Peaches, apples, and plums.

What do you want?
    I want an apple.

Peaches, apples, and plums.

Let's Learn

What do you want?
  I want some ice cream.
  I want some cake and some ice cream.

62

Practise.

milk

fish

chicken

pizza

bread

rice

cake

ice cream

Say these.

I want _____ and _____ .

Let's Learn Some More

Do you want some chicken?
Yes, I do.
No, I do not.

do not = don't

Practise.

 Let's Learn the Alphabet

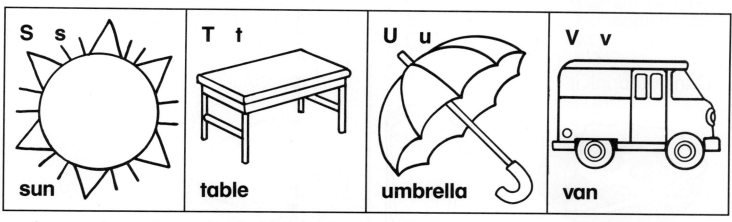

a b c d e f g h i j k l m n o p q r s t u v w x y z

Let's Move

I'm buying an apple.

I'm washing it.

I'm cutting it.

I'm eating it.

I'm buying some juice.

I'm opening it.

I'm pouring it.

I'm drinking it.

Can you drink it?

Can you eat it?

66

 **Let's Listen**

1.

2.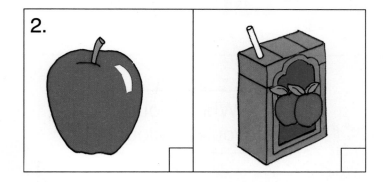

3.

4.

5.

6.

7.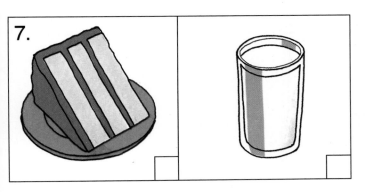

8.

Unit Eight

Let's Talk

What is your favourite colour?
Red.

What is = What's

Let's Sing

♪ What Do You Like?

I like yellow, yes I do.
I like yellow, yes I do.
I like yellow.
    I do, too.
    I like yellow, too.

I like ice cream, yes I do.
I like ice cream, yes I do.
I like ice cream.
    I do, too.
    I like ice cream, too.

I like tennis, yes I do.
I like tennis, yes I do.
I like tennis, ~~yes I do~~.
    I do, too.
    I like tennis, too.

Let's Learn

What do you like?
I like frogs.
I like frogs, too.

70

Practise.

There's a bird.
I like birds.
I like birds, too.

a bird	birds	a dog	dogs	a cat	cats

a frog	frogs	a rabbit	rabbits	a spider	spiders

Ask your partner.

What do you like?

Let's Learn Some More

Do you like spiders?
Yes, I do.
No, I do not.

do not = don't

Practise.

Do you like robots?

No, I don't.

 # Let's Learn the Alphabet

W w	X x	Y y	Z z
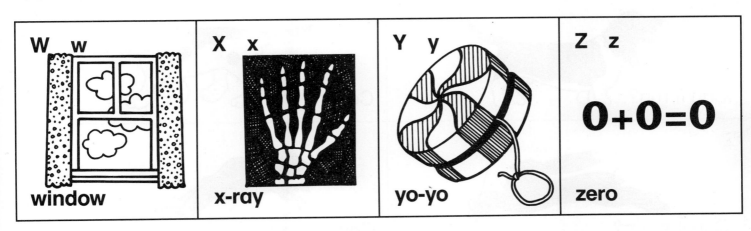			0+0=0
window	x-ray	yo-yo	zero

a b c d e f g h i j k l m n o p q r s t u v **w x y z**

Let's Move

I'm walking.

I'm running.

I'm swimming.

I'm flying.

I'm hopping.

I'm jumping.

Can it run?
Yes, it can.
No, it cannot.

cannot = can't

Can it run?

Can it fly?

Can it swim?

Can it hop?

Let's Listen

1.

2.

3.

4.

5.

6.

7.

8.

Let's Review

1. Say these.

10 POINTS

2. Answer the question.

What do you want?

3. Say and act.

4. Ask your partner.

Do you like _____?

5. Listen carefully.

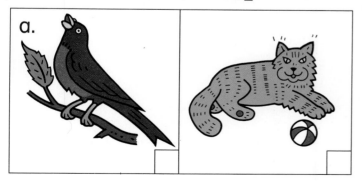

Syllabus

UNIT	LANGUAGE ITEMS	FUNCTIONS	TOPICS
1	Hello, I am (Andy). Hi! My name is (Kate). What's your name? What's this? It's (a book). Is this (a book)? Yes, it is. No, it isn't.	Greetings Introducing yourself Asking someone's name Asking about objects (singular) Identifying objects (singular) Classroom commands	Names Classroom objects
2	How are you? I'm fine, thank you. What colour is it? It's (red). This is a (blue) (book). This is a (red) and (yellow) book.	Greetings Asking about colours Identifying colours Describing objects Classroom commands	Colours Classroom objects
3	This is my friend, (Sarah). Hello, (Sarah). Let's play. What are these? They're (cassettes). How many (trainers)? (Ten) (trainers).	Introducing friends Suggesting an activity Asking about objects (plural) Identifying objects (plural) Asking about numbers Counting 1–10 Classroom commands	Numbers 1–10 Classroom objects
4	Hi, Mum! I'm home. This is my (mother). It's nice to meet you. It's nice to meet you, too. Who's (she)? (She's) my (grandmother). (She's) (short). Don't (watch TV).	Introducing family members Meeting someone politely Asking about people Identifying people Describing people Negative commands	Family
5	Happy birthday, (Jenny)! How old are you? I'm (seven) years old. This is for you. It's (my) birthday today. What is it? I don't know. It's (little). It's a (little) (yo-yo). Can you (play with a yo-yo)? Yes, I can. No, I can't.	Birthday greetings Asking and telling age Giving a gift Guessing Describing objects Asking about ability	Birthdays Age Toys

UNIT	LANGUAGE ITEMS	FUNCTIONS	TOPICS
6	Is the (sun) (shining)? Is the (sun) (shining) now? No, it's (raining). The (sun) is (shining). How many (clouds) are there? There are (six) (clouds). There's one (cloud). Where's the (kite)? It's (in) the tree. Where are the (books)? They're (under) the (table). I'm (climbing a tree). Is he (climbing a tree)?	Asking about the weather Describing the weather Counting Describing a situation Asking about location Specifying location Asking about ability	Weather Outdoor activities
7	I'm (hungry). I want (an apple). Here you are. Thank you. You're welcome. What do you want? I want (some cake) and (some ice cream). Do you want (some chicken)? Yes, I do. No, I don't. I'm (buying) (an apple). I'm (washing) it.	Expressing hunger and thirst Asking what someone wants Expressing wants Logical sequencing	Food and drink
8	What's your favourite colour? (Red). What do you like? I like (blue). I like (frogs). I like (frogs), too. Do you like (spiders)? Yes, I do. No, I don't. I'm (walking). Can it (swim)? Yes, it can. No, it can't.	Asking about favourites Expressing likes Agreeing Asking about ability	Favourite colours Animals

Word List

A
a 8
alphabet 11
am 6
an 9
and 18
apple 19
are 14
at 20
away 20

B
baby 35
bag 9
ball 45
be 12
bicycle 45
big 46
bird 71
birthday 42
black 17
blowing 51
blue 17
board 20
book 9
box 46
boy 30
bread 63
brother 33
brown 17
buying 66
by 54

C
cake 62
can 48
cannot 48
can't 48
car 45
carefully 12
cassette 26
cat 8
catch 48
chair 9
chicken 63
circle 30
climbing 56
close 12
cloud 52
colour 16
come 30
count 30
crayon 27
cutting 66

D
day 51
desk 9
dinner 38
do 38
dog 70
doll 44
don't 38
door 30
down 12
draw 30
drink 66
drinking 66

E
eat 38
eating 66
egg 29
eight 28
English 11
eraser 9

F
family 33
fat 36
father 33
favourite 68
fine 14
fish 29
five 28
flower 53
fly 74
flying 56
for 42
four 28
friend 24
frog 70

G
girl 30
give 30
go out 51
go to 30
good morning 38
good night 38
grandfather 34
grandmother 34
grey 17
green 17

H
hand 20
Happy birthday 42
he 34
he's 34
hello 6
here 30
hi 6
hit 48
home 32
homework 38
hop 74
hopping 74
house 37
how 14
hungry 60

I
I 6
ice cream 62
I'm 14
in 54
ink 37
is 6
isn't 10
it 8
it's 8

J
jeans 37
juice 60
jumping 74

K
kick 48
kite 45
know 44

L
let's 24
like 11
line 30
lion 47
listen 12
little 46
long 46
look 20

M
make 30
many 28
marker 27
me 30
meet 32
mess 38
milk 63
mother 32
my 6

N
name 6
nice 32
nine 28
no 10
not 10
notebook 27
now 43

O
octopus 55
oh 51
old 36
on 54
one 28
open 12
opening 66
orange 17
out 20

P
peach 61
pen 9
pencil 9
pencil case 26
piano 38
pick up 20
picture 30
pink 17
pizza 63
play 24
playing 56
please 12
plum 61
point to 12
pouring 66
pretty 36
puddle 53
purple 17
put away 20
put down 20
put up 20
puzzle 45

Q
question 55
quiet 12

R
rabbit 71
racket 45
raining 50
rainy 51
reading 56
red 16

rice 63
riding 56
robot 42
round 46
ruler 8
run 74
running 74

S
seven 28
she 34
she's 34
shining 50
short 36
sister 33
sit down 12
six 28
skip 48
skipping rope 45
sleep 38
snowing 51
snowy 51
some 60
song 7
spider 71
square 46
stand up 12
sun 50
sunny 51
swim 74
swimming 74

T
table 27
tag 56
take out 20
tall 36
teacher 12
ten 28
tennis 56
thank you 14
the 12
there 52
there's 52
these 26
they 26
they're 26
thin 36
thirsty 60
this 8
three 28
tidy up 38
to 12
today 43
too 32
touch 12
trainer 28
tree 53

TV 38
two 28

U
ugly 36
umbrella 65
under 54
up 12

V
van 65

W
wake up 38
walking 74
want 60
washing 66
watch 38
welcome 60
what 6
what's 6
where 54
where's 54
white 17
who 34
who's 34
wind 51
window 73
windy 51
with 48
wow 42
write 20

X
x-ray 73

Y
years 42
yellow 17
yes 10
yo-yo 45
you 14
young 36
your 6
you're 43

Z
zero 73